Anim

Written by Jo Windsor

Rigby

Look at this animal.
It is a glowworm.
A glowworm has
a light in its tail.

This cave has lots
of glowworms in it.
The glowworms
look like little stars.

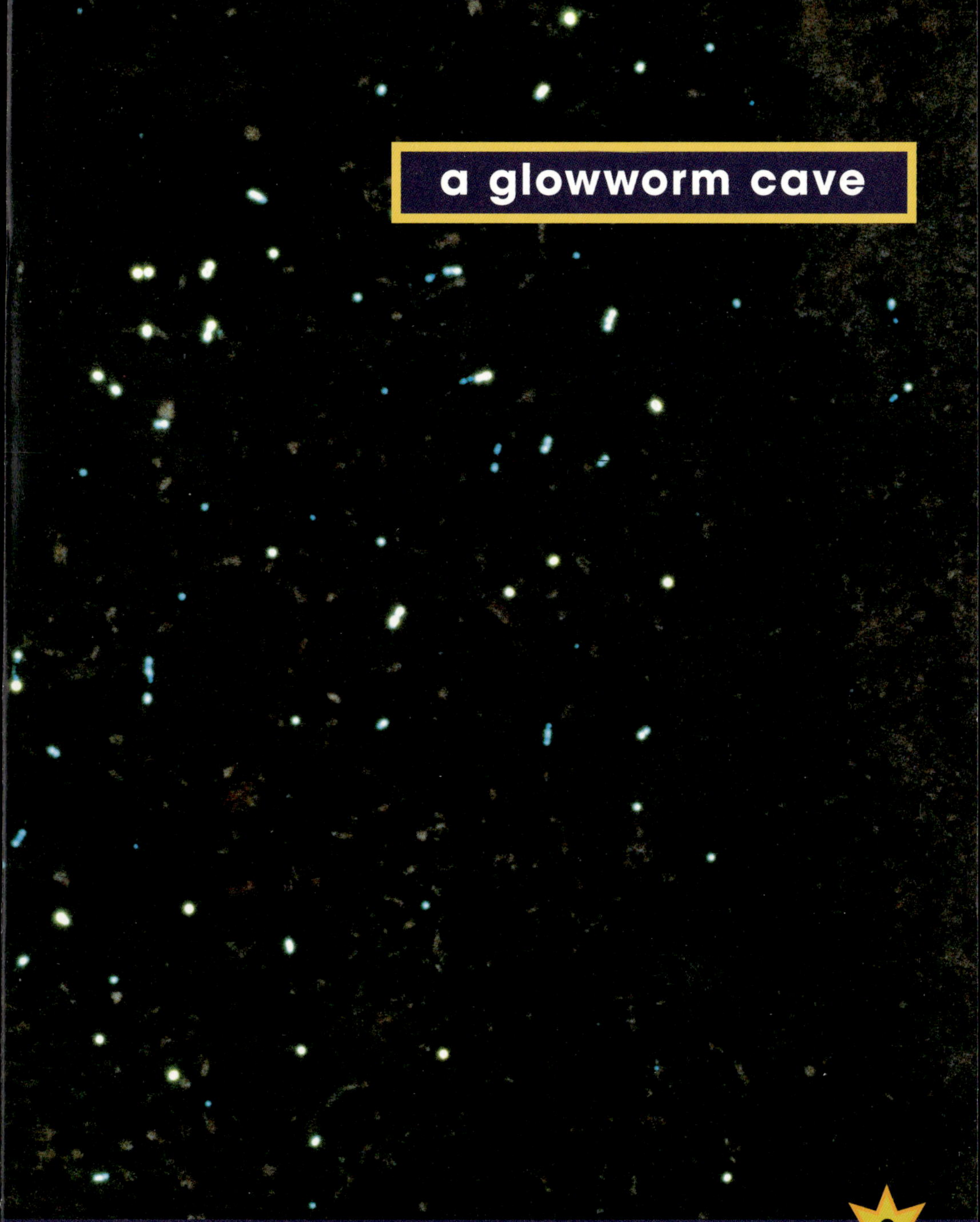
a glowworm cave

Here is a firefly.
A firefly has a light
in its tail, too.
The light in its tail
can go on and off.

Some fish have
lights to help them
get food.
This fish has lights
on its body.
It has lights
under its body, too.

Look at this fish.
It has a light
under its eye.

The light is
under a flap.
The fish can open
and shut the flap.
When the flap
is open, the light
will come on.

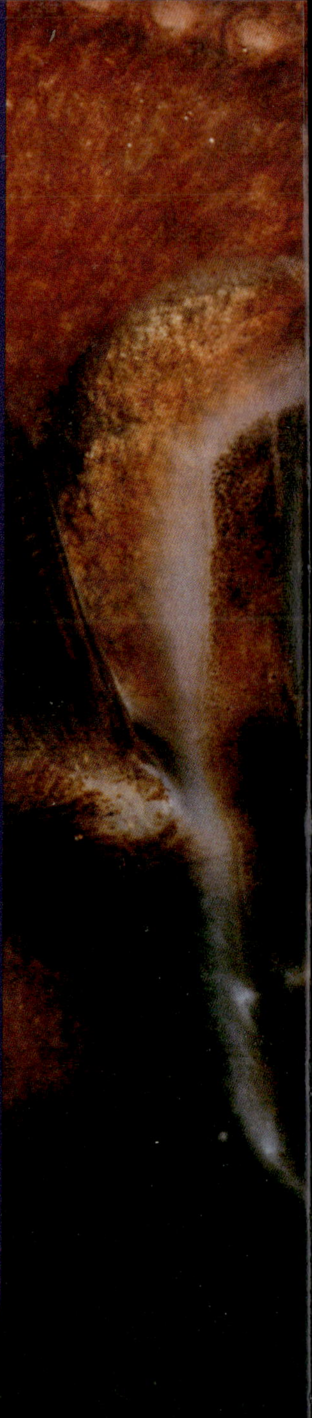

This fish has
lights, too.
It has lights
on its body
and its mouth.

The lights help it
to get food.

Look at this fish.
This fish lives down,
down in the sea.
It has lots of lights
on its body.

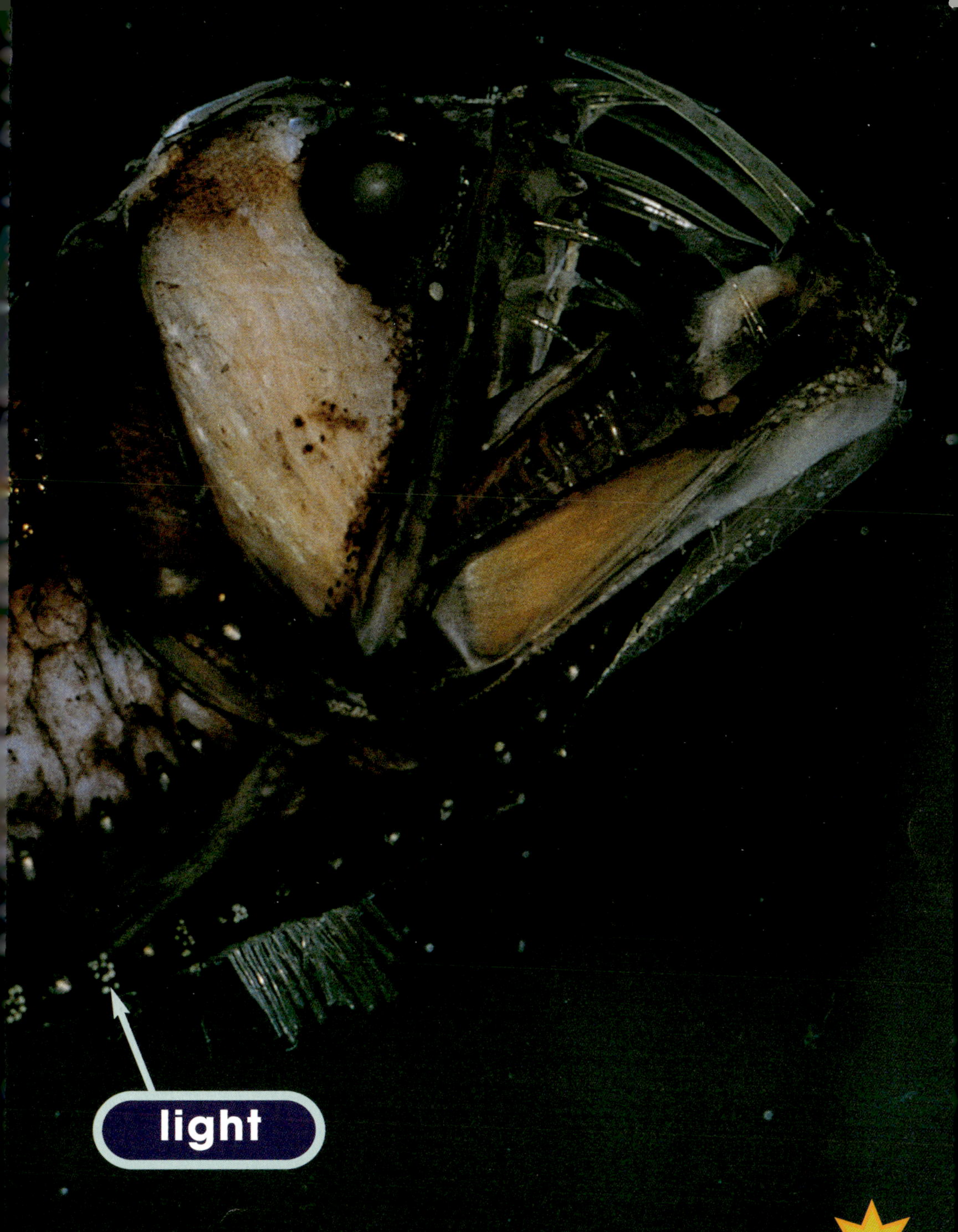
light

The big fish has
a light on its head.
The light helps it
to get little fish
to eat.

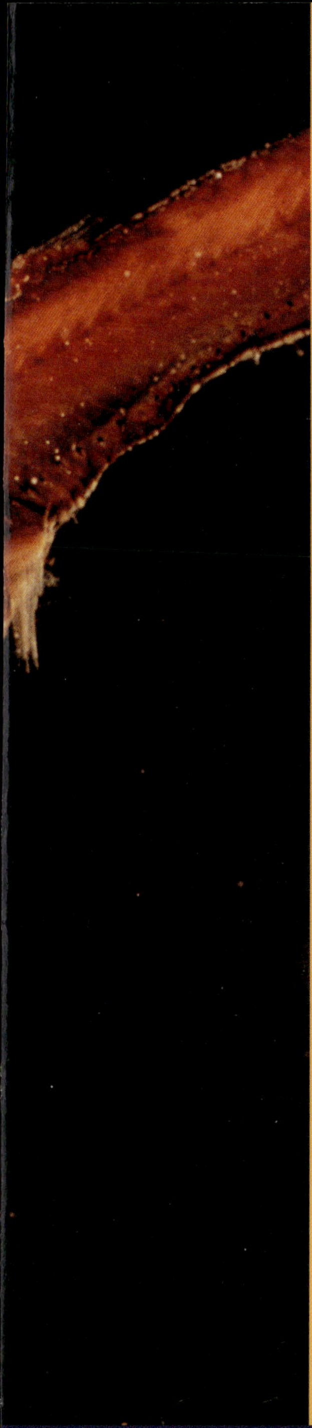

Index

Guide Notes

Title: Animal Lights
Stage: Early (3) – Blue

Genre: Nonfiction (Expository)
Approach: Guided Reading
Processes: Thinking Critically, Exploring Language, Processing Information
Written and Visual Focus: Photographs (static images), Captions, Labels, Index

Thinking Critically

(sample questions)

- Look at the front cover and read the title. Ask the children: "What do you think this book could be about?"
- Ask the children what animals they know that have lights.
- Focus the children's attention on the Index. Ask: "What are you going to find out about in this book?"
- If you want to find out about lights on bodies, on which pages would you look?
- If you want to find out about lights in tails, on which pages would you look?
- Look at pages 2 and 3. Why do you think glowworms live in a cave?
- Look at pages 4 and 5. When do you think the lights on the fireflies' tails would go off?
- Look at pages 10 and 11. How do you think the lights help the fish to get food?

Exploring Language

Terminology

Title, cover, photographs, author, photographers

Vocabulary

Interest words: glowworm, stars, firefly, light
High-frequency words (new): has, off, lots
Compound word: glowworm
Positional words: under, down

Print Conventions

Capital letter for sentence beginnings, periods, commas